My Encounter with
IDENTITY CRISIS

A Journey from Doubt to Self - Discovery

TANYA KUMARI

ISBN
Paperback 979-8-89724-567-3
Hardcase 979-8-89744-987-3

A broken glass, a fleeting gaze,
The pieces don't align,
What's seen is not the whole truth,
A puzzle left behind.

Prologue

The Quiet Storm

It's strange how life can change in the blink of an eye; how, one moment, you're perfectly content with the person you are, and the next, you're standing in front of a mirror questioning everything you once took for granted.

I remember the first time I truly saw myself differently. It wasn't a dramatic event, but rather a subtle shift, like the sky gradually darkening before a storm. The kind of storm that doesn't show its full force right away, but quietly chips away at your sense of self, leaving you adrift in a sea of doubt.

There's something disorienting about the feeling of losing yourself, of watching the world around you continue as if nothing has changed, while internally, you're grappling with your own reflection. Everyone sees what's on the outside, but it's what's inside that's truly at war. It's an inner battle most people can't see, but it's the one that matters most.

What happens when you stop believing in the person you've always been? What happens when the world starts telling you you're not enough, even when you don't know how to ask for help? This book isn't just about my struggle with my reflection. It's about the invisible battles we face when we lose our confidence and how, even when you can't see the way forward, there's always a way to rebuild.

Author's Note

Dear Reader,

As you turn these pages, you might wonder why I've chosen to share such personal moments of my life, moments I once thought I'd keep hidden forever. Writing this book was not easy. In fact, at times, it felt like I was exposing pieces of myself that I wasn't ready to confront. But there comes a time in every story, whether it's the one you're living or the one you're reading, when the truth becomes the most powerful tool of all.

This book is more than just a collection of memories. It's a mirror to my past, a journey that shaped who I am today - flaws, fears, and all. It's the story of a girl who thought she had everything under control, only to realize that control was never the answer. It's about learning to embrace the imperfections, the struggles, and the quiet moments of self-doubt that everyone faces but few openly acknowledge.

I share my story with you in hopes that you find comfort in the truth. That you recognize pieces of yourself in these words, knowing that you're not alone in your own battles. If there's anything I've learned through all of this, it's that healing begins when we allow ourselves to be seen, in all of our rawness.

To those of you who have ever felt lost, uncertain, or unworthy; this book is for you. And if you've ever wondered whether things will get better, let me tell you this: the answer is yes. There's always hope, even on the darkest days. Thank you for reading, for walking alongside me through this journey of rediscovery. May this book remind you that you are enough, just as you are.

With love and gratitude,

Tanya Kumari

A Personal Message to You

Before you dive into the pages ahead, I just want to take a moment to speak directly to you. I know that picking up a book like this requires trust. You're letting me into your space, and I want to honor that. The story you're about to read is deeply personal, and I'm offering it to you not as a finished work of someone who has it all figured out, but as a raw, honest reflection of a journey that is still unfolding.

As you read, please know that I'm not expecting you to have all the answers. I'm not even sure I do. But what I do know is that sharing this with you is part of my own healing, an invitation for you to join me, if you so choose, in embracing the uncertainties and imperfections of life.

And if my words resonate with you, if they stir something inside, I hope you'll find comfort in knowing that you're not alone. In this world, we often feel isolated in our struggles, but the truth is, we're all walking this path together, searching, learning, growing, and stumbling along the way.

So, take your time. Let this story sink in, and let it remind you that no matter where you are on your own journey, it's okay to not have everything figured out. You are exactly where you need to be and I'm so glad you're here.

With you.

Contents

Contents

I wore my armor in the form of a smile,
Hiding the storms that brewed all the while.
The world moved forward, unaware,
Of the weight I carried, the silent despair.
But beneath the cracks, a light still burned,
A spark of hope that I had yet to learn.
For in the darkness, I began to see,
The reflection I feared was still part of me.
I write these words, not for praise or fame,
But for the truth, for the healing of the flame.
We are more than our scars, more than our pain,
And even the broken can rise again.

Chapter 1

Shattered Reflections

I stood in front of the mirror, my breath coming in sharp gasps. The reflection staring back at me was a stranger's. Her hollow eyes, the acne - scarred skin, the lifelessness in her posture, none of it was familiar. She wasn't me, but somehow, she was all that was left of who I had once been. A 16-year-old girl, who had once been confident and admired, now felt like a ghost in her own life.

It hadn't always been this way. I remember a time when my world was full of light. I was the girl everyone noticed, the one who smiled effortlessly and made everyone feel good just by walking into a room. Compliments were second nature to me. My friends adored me. Teachers praised me for my brilliance. My relatives constantly called me beautiful. Life had been simple, and I hadn't thought much about who I was beyond those easy labels. I had no reason to doubt myself.

But that girl - the one I had been was slipping away, and I didn't know how to stop it.

At first, the changes came so slowly, I didn't notice them. But they were there, creeping into my life in subtle ways. My skin, once clear and glowing, betrayed me. Small, red bumps started to appear, and no matter how many products I tried, they only seemed to get worse. The more I tried to hide them, the more they spread, turning my face into a map of my insecurities. It was hard to look in the mirror without feeling like I was looking at a stranger.

And it wasn't just my face. My body, my entire being, was changing in ways I couldn't control. I'd find myself staring at my hands, almost as if they belonged to someone else. They had become so thin, so frail, like fragile branches that could snap with the slightest pressure.

When had they lost their strength? When had they become so delicate, so *insubstantial?*

The truth hit me like a punch to the gut: it was the anxiety, the constant fear gnawing at me from the inside. Every moment spent locked in my own head, the spiraling with doubt and self-loathing. I started pushing the food away, making it feel like eating was something I didn't deserve, something I couldn't even enjoy anymore.

The changes didn't just show on my face, they were everywhere, a silent force that twisted me into something I couldn't even recognize. My body was being overtaken by something invisible, something I could feel with every breath, every glance in the mirror. It was like I was at war with myself, fighting a battle I didn't understand and couldn't escape from. And the worst part?

"It was nothing but my hormones, those treacherous hormones that were wreaking havoc in ways I couldn't even begin to comprehend. They were shifting, changing me, shaping me into a version of myself that I couldn't control. My body was betraying me, and I had no way of stopping it.

My family - humble and loving, could see my pain. They could feel the weight of my frustration, the desperation in my eyes as each day passed. They tried everything. No remedy was too extreme, no suggestion too outlandish.

I ate twenty-five neem leaves raw, day after day, because someone, had told me it would make my skin clear. I slathered every cream, every concoction I could find on my face, desperate for relief, hoping it would fix what felt like a punishment I didn't deserve. They did what they could. They wanted to fix me, to make me whole again, to help me reclaim the girl who had once walked through life with confidence.

But the truth was more brutal than any of us realized. None of it worked. Nothing could fix what was happening to me. Hormones. The root of it all. My body was changing at lightning speed, puberty crashing through me like a storm. I could see it in the mirror, feel it in my bones. One minute, I was losing weight uncontrollably, shrinking before my own eyes, and the next, my skin was covered in angry, red bumps, laughing at every chemical treatment I put on them.

My family despite their best efforts, couldn't fix what they didn't fully understand. They took me to the dermatologist, but I knew deep down, that those treatments would take time to show results. And when your hormones are flipping your world upside down at a speed you can't keep up with? Time wasn't on my side.

We were a middle-class family, doing our best with what we had. They gave everything they could, scraping together what little money they had to take me to a doctor, but nothing could change the fact that the real battle wasn't with the creams or the pills. It was with my own body, fighting against me in a war I couldn't win. It wasn't just everything else, it was my mind, too. I was trapped in this whirlwind of hormones, of emotions, of changes that were beyond my control.

I wasn't me anymore.

My friends didn't seem to notice. Or maybe they didn't care. I remember one afternoon, sitting with them in the cafeteria, trying to push the uncomfortable feeling in my chest aside. They were chatting about someone else, about their beauty, their perfect skin, how they always looked put together.

"She's flawless," one of them said, and I could feel the words cut through me.

They weren't even looking at me, but it was like I could hear the unspoken comparison in their voices. The silence that followed was deafening.

I could feel myself shrinking, trapped in a room full of faces that no longer saw me. I tried to smile, but it felt like a mask I wasn't sure how to wear anymore.

Then came the comments. My emotions, once as steady as my old confidence, were unpredictable.

"What happened to her face?" I overheard my aunt say at a family gathering, her voice too loud, too cruel.

"She's ruining her looks with all that acne."

I wanted to scream, to explain that this wasn't something I could control. But the words never came. Instead, I stopped looking in the mirror, and I stopped trusting my reflection.

I started to believe that maybe I wasn't enough, that the girl I had been, was lost, and the girl standing in front of the mirror was a shadow of that person.

I started becoming more aware of the little things that made me uncomfortable, like the lice. It wasn't a huge deal, really. A lot of schoolgirls go through it. But for me, it felt like just another thing on top of everything else.

There was that one moment, though. That one moment that left me questioning everything.

So when my best friend casually said,

"Your hair stinks", it felt like a slap across my face.

I froze. For a split second, I didn't know how to respond. It hit harder than I expected. It was a joke, right? She couldn't be serious. But the laughter in her voice cut deeper than she realized.

It wasn't just the hair. It was that I was already so conscious of myself, so aware of everything I felt, was wrong. Lice, infections, acne, it all made me feel like I was falling apart. And that comment? It felt like the cherry on the cake, the final blow, reminding me that I wasn't good enough.

I wanted to hide. I wanted to run. But I just smiled weakly, pretending it didn't hurt. Inside, I was dying. I touched my hair, feeling the strands as if they too had turned against me. Was this how people saw me now?

Something… disgusting?

But the real battle wasn't external. It was what was happening inside me, in places where no one could see. The more I tried to focus on my studies, the harder it became.

I used to love school, my grades had been my refuge. But now, every time I opened a book, all I could think about was how my face looked in the reflection of the window, how my clothes felt too tight or too loose. I couldn't escape the constant thoughts that consumed me.

I started to spiral. My grades slipped, my attention fractured. I couldn't concentrate on anything. Every test, every exam, felt like a mountain I couldn't climb. I wasn't worried about my studies anymore. I was worried about how to cover the acne on my face or which hairstyle would hide the puffiness I had developed.

And then, TV became my escape. Of course, to only make things worse.

I would find myself sitting in front of the screen for hours, watching people who seemed to have everything together. They were perfect. Beautiful, with flawless skin and radiant smiles that looked like they belonged to a world I could never touch. They were happy, effortlessly so. Their lives seemed to shine with everything I felt I had lost. And as I watched them, I couldn't help but compare myself to them.

I would catch glimpses of my reflection in the TV screen - and then I would look back at them, wondering how I had become so... ordinary. So invisible.

Sometimes I would think, if only I could look like them, like those people on TV. Maybe then, people would see me again. Maybe then, I wouldn't feel so alone. Maybe then, I would stop feeling like I was disappearing, as if everyone around me had forgotten I existed.

But the more I watched, the more it became clear:

"I wasn't like them. And maybe, I never could be."

The world around me didn't make it any easier. The people in my life, the ones who had once lifted me up, now seemed like strangers. Even my teachers, who had always supported me, didn't seem to notice when I stopped trying. They didn't see the girl who had once been a star student, the girl who could do anything. They only saw the girl who was slowly fading into the background.

But then, something unexpected happened.

One day, in the middle of class, I felt it. A gaze. A weight pressing against my chest. I glanced up and caught him; my classmate, the quiet boy who sat across from me in Physics class. He wasn't someone I'd ever really noticed before, but his eyes were locked on mine. It was like he was staring right through me, and yet, at the same time, I felt like he could see something I hadn't seen in years.

My heart started racing. What was he doing? I looked away quickly, but the tension in the air was palpable. He never looked at me like that, no one did anymore. And yet, there he was, staring at me as if he saw more than just the reflection of my flaws.

The bell rang, but he didn't get up like the others. Instead, he stood up slowly, his hands shaking, and made his way towards my desk. My pulse quickened. What was he doing? What did he want?

He stopped in front of me, avoiding my gaze. His voice was barely above a whisper.

"I… I like you," he muttered, shifting uncomfortably.

I froze. The words hung in the air, but I couldn't move.

"I've liked you for a long time", he added, his face turning bright red.

I couldn't believe what I was hearing. How could he like me? Me, with all my imperfections, my self-doubt? How could anyone like someone as broken as I was?

I wanted to respond, to ask him how he could possibly see anything worth liking in me. But the words didn't come. Instead, all I could do was stare at him, feeling the weight of his confession crash into me.

I ran. I didn't think about it, I just bolted. My heart was pounding, my head spinning. I had to get away. Away from the reflection that haunted me. Away from the boy who somehow saw something in me that I couldn't see in myself.

I slammed the door behind me when I got home, I thought maybe the world would stop spinning. But it didn't. Instead, I locked myself in my room, sinking to the floor as the tears came crashing out, uncontrollable. I wasn't crying because of him, not because he had confessed his feelings. No!

I cried because it was too much to process, too impossible to believe. How could someone ever care for someone like *me*? The girl with acne and doubts and walls built so high, I couldn't see beyond them.

I cried because it felt like a cruel joke that someone *actually* wanted me, but how could they, when all I saw was a mess of insecurities and flaws? How could anyone see anything good in the broken, unworthy person I felt I was?

I felt suffocated by the weight of my own self-doubt, my reflection mocking me with every tear. I couldn't make sense of it.

In that moment, all I could think was:

"How could someone see beauty in something so broken?"

I had no answers.

But even in that moment of darkness, something inside me started to stir. The girl I once was, the confident, proud girl was still there. Buried under layers of doubt and self-loathing, but not gone. Not yet.

Maybe I didn't have all the answers, but I knew one thing:

I wasn't done. I was still here.

And just as I wiped my tears, trying to piece myself back together, there was a knock at the door.

My heart stopped.

The knock on the door shattered the silence.

I hesitated, unsure of who it could be. The familiar rhythm of the world had felt so far away, and yet now, the stillness was being disrupted. I stood still, the quiet pressing in around me.

It wasn't just the knock. It was the sense that something new was on the other side, something that could change everything. But who was it? What did they want? Could this moment finally be the beginning of something else?

I walked slowly towards the door, each step heavier than the last. The uncertainty gnawed at me. But I couldn't help it. This was the moment. The next chapter. The phase I had been waiting for, even if I hadn't known it until now.

And as I reached the door, my hand trembling slightly on the handle, I knew one thing.

I was ready to face whatever came next.

The End... or is it?

Sometimes, we are trapped in the spaces between
moments. Caught between the past that no longer fits
and the future we can't touch.

We wait…

Not for answers, but for the courage to move forward.

The knock may be silent, but its echo is deafening.
The door may remain closed, but its weight presses
down on our chest.

Sometimes, the hardest part isn't facing what's ahead.
It's deciding if we're ready to leave what's behind.

Chapter 2

One Step Forward

The knock

It haunted me, echoing through my mind like an unanswered question. I couldn't stop thinking about it. The weight of it, the pause before I opened the door. Had I been waiting for something? Or was I afraid of what I'd find on the other side?

I never opened it. I didn't even move.

For days, I wondered what would have happened if I had answered. Who was on the other side? What was I supposed to do? But the moment never returned. It was gone, like everything else in my life, fading, slipping away, leaving me with the sense that I'd missed something important, something life-changing.

Instead, I found myself facing something else entirely.

The knock at the door felt like the end of one chapter, but it was only the beginning of another –

COLLEGE.

It had always been a dream, hadn't it? To get through school, excel, make it to the next level, and find my place in the world. But somewhere between the overbearing pressure of perfection and the constant fight with my own self-worth, that dream had become a nightmare.

In school, I had once been that girl; flawless grades, confident, the one everyone expected to succeed. But by the time I reached 12th grade, I couldn't even recognize my reflection in the marks I was receiving. It wasn't just the grades. It was everything.

I couldn't believe those were my marks. My teachers couldn't either. The once-praised student, the one who had it all together, was suddenly slipping through the cracks. I had once been a star, on top of the world in the one area that had always been my comfort zone. Now, I had turned pale, unsure, and unprepared for the fact that everything was unraveling.

Those months leading up to my final exams felt like a fog I couldn't escape. The weight of expectations pressed down on me like a physical force. Each day felt longer than the last, and my health, both physical and mental, deteriorated slowly but surely. The late nights of studying, the constant overthinking, the dread that kept me awake, everything had taken its toll. I was crumbling from the inside, and I didn't know how to stop it.

I was so lost in my own mind that I would read a page ten times, but the words would blur together, refusing to make sense. I could feel the knowledge slipping through my fingers, but no matter how hard I tried, I couldn't grasp it. The pages, once filled with promises of success, now seemed like a foreign language, mocking me with their impenetrability. Each sentence felt impossible, and I didn't have the energy to push through.

After the results came in, I sat alone at home. The house was too quiet, too still. But my mind..my mind was anything but quiet. It buzzed, restless, relentless. I couldn't escape the spiraling thoughts.

"Is it worth it?"

I asked myself, staring at the walls, but seeing nothing. Was the pressure, the stress, the toll on my body and soul, really changing anything? Had it made me a better person, a better student? Or had it just made me miserable?

"Can I change what happened until now?"

No.

"But can I change what happens next?"

Sure.

In that moment of clarity, I felt something shift within me. The darkness didn't just evaporate, but the weight I'd been carrying for so long started to feel a little lighter. I could let go. I didn't have to keep dragging the past with me. I couldn't change what had happened, but I had the power to shape what was ahead.

So, I decided. I would bring myself together. I would stop dwelling on past mistakes and fears. I would focus on what lay ahead on the next chapter - the one that was yet to be written.

Summer passed in a blur of uncertainty and anticipation. The pressure, though, never really left. It was time to think about college, about the future that everyone else seemed so sure of. Everyone around me was excited, discussing where they could go, which college they wanted to join, and who would follow which stream. The air was thick with plans, with certainty, with the shared belief that the next step would be simple, easy.

But for me, it wasn't. The choice felt like a heavy fog I couldn't see through. I had two paths in front of me, and neither felt clear.

1. I could join a nearby college with all my friends, my safety net, my comfort zone.

(or)

2. I could go to a college 50 kilometers away from the city, a place where I knew absolutely no one.

The second option terrified me. I had grown comfortable in my bubble and stepping out of it felt like leaping into the unknown. But that's what made it the choice that mattered. The first option, staying in the comfort zone, staying with my friends seemed safe, but it didn't excite me. It didn't challenge me.

So I thought. And thought. And thought some more.

Each option seemed to weigh down on me. If I stayed, I would have the comfort of my friends, the familiar faces, the safety of my past. But if I left... I had no idea what waited for me. I was terrified of what being alone would mean. Terrified of the unknown.

"What if I failed?"

"What if I couldn't handle it?"

"What if I lost myself completely?"

I knew this decision would change everything. Where I went to college would shape my entire future. The people I'd meet, the experiences I'd have, the path I would take, it all depended on this one choice.

The thought of going somewhere alone to a place where I didn't know anyone, made my heart race. But then, a quiet voice within me whispered, Maybe this is what you need. Maybe it wasn't about the friends I had or the life I was clinging to. Maybe it was about finally stepping outside of my fears, outside of my insecurities, and seeing how I would stand on my own.

My family, ever supportive, left the decision entirely up to me. They didn't pressurize me, didn't try to sway me one way or the other. I could feel the weight of their trust, but it didn't make the decision any easier.

In the end, I made a decision. A decision that changed my life forever. And now, looking back, I'm thankful to the old version of myself for making it.

I decided to leave my comfort zone behind. I chose the college far away, the one where I knew no one… absolutely no one. It was a decision that made my heart pound in fear and excitement at the same time. I had no idea what awaited me there, but I knew one thing for sure: it was time for me to reclaim my confidence.

It wasn't just a college choice anymore. It felt like I was stepping away from everything that had shaped me. The friends who had once been my world, the expectations that were now crumbling, leaving them behind felt both - freeing and suffocating. But deep down, I knew this was the only way forward. To find myself, I had to leave what I thought was home.

But before I could truly understand that, before I could accept what was to come, I had to face myself. My mind was in a blur, full of questions, doubts, and fears I couldn't even explain.

I was questioning everything, my choices, my identity, my worth. In those moments of overwhelming silence, when no one was around to judge or offer their opinions, I found myself reflecting... in the rawest form.

The confusion, the anger, the pain, they all swirled within me, making it harder to breathe. But in the end, the only place where I could be completely honest with myself was in the quiet of my thoughts.

So, I wrote –

"Dear Diary,

How are you today?

I don't know how I am, really. I'm supposed to be fine, right?

At least, that's what I tell myself every morning. But am I really? I don't think so.

Since the results came out, I've been feeling lost. Today, I'm here because I've to make a big decision - college.

I can either go with my friends to a nearby college, or I can take a chance and go to that far away college, which has better exposure, but where I don't know anyone. I will have to travel alone, sit alone, make friends from scratch.

Oh my god!

It feels like a choice between comfort and fear. But I also wonder that - Even my friends couldn't help me find my confidence. What if strangers do? Is it worth the risk? What if I make the wrong choice? What if I regret it? What if, just what if… I blame myself?

Maybe it's time to try something different. Maybe it's time for a change.

I'm scared. But, I'll still have to figure it out on my own.

See you, Diary."

I couldn't escape myself, but I could escape the environment that was suffocating me. I had to take the leap.

And so, I did. I stepped into a world of strangers, a place where no one knew my past, my insecurities, or my failures. It was just me, facing the world, facing myself in the rawest form possible.

Was I happy with the decision I made?

Yes. Absolutely.

Looking back now, I know that decision was the turning point in my life. It's what set me on the path to becoming who I am today.

The uncertainty, the fear of the unknown, all of it, was like a storm I had no choice but to walk through. But I had to take that step, no matter how daunting it seemed at the time. And though I couldn't have known it then, stepping out of my comfort zone would not just change my future, it would force me to change myself.

I had worked so hard to make things better. I had started taking care of my health, listening to medical advice, and taking small steps towards improvement. I was getting better, at least physically. But my impatience, my relentless desire for quick fixes, had kept me from truly growing.

I was as eager as a child, wanting everything to fall into place faster than it could. And yet, no matter how much I tried, my confidence remained a fragile thing, as shaky as it had always been.

The first day of college -

The day I'd been dreading and anticipating at the same time. A place that was 50 kilometers away from the comfort of home, surrounded by faces I had never seen, voices I had never heard. A new world.

But for me, it felt more like a test. I felt like an imposter, walking into a room full of strangers. Every step I took, I could hear the loud, insistent voice in my head:

"They will judge you. They will see you for who you were, not who you are. They will look at your appearance and think you're not enough."

But there was one thing I clung to, *"they don't know me."*

They don't know how broken I was, how far I've come, how much I've struggled. And because of that, maybe they won't judge me the way people from my past had. Maybe, just maybe, I could escape the whispers of my past self.

I stood in front of the mirror that morning, heart pounding in my chest, my emotions, a storm I couldn't quite tame. Excitement mixed with fear, hope tangled with anxiety, and somewhere beneath it all, a deep sense of loneliness.

"What if I don't belong there? What if they look at me and see everything I've been trying to leave behind?"

The drive to college felt like a thousand miles. A place I had been dreaming about for so long, yet when I finally arrived, it was nothing like I had imagined. Surrounded by people who spoke in accents I couldn't quite place, faces I didn't recognize, I felt... small. Like a leaf floating aimlessly in an ocean of strangers.

I felt lost, out of place. Everyone else seemed so comfortable, so confident. I couldn't stop comparing myself to them, feeling inferior with each passing moment.

The first day dragged on. And no, it wasn't the people who made me feel out of place. They were kind, friendly even, but it was me who couldn't fit in. My mind kept racing.

"Why can't I just be normal? Why do I feel like I don't belong here?"

I was searching for someone, anyone, I knew, but all I saw were unfamiliar faces, and it only made me feel more isolated. One week went by, and I pushed myself to keep going. But by the end of it, I couldn't fight the weight of it anymore. I broke.

Coming from the northern part of India, adjusting to a whole new world in the South was harder than I had imagined. I had always loved this place, but this was the first time I was surrounded by locals who didn't understand the awkwardness I carried with me. Just as much as I wasn't used to them, they weren't used to me.

Then, that moment came, the one that crushed everything. It was a day like any other, sitting in class, pretending to be normal, pretending that everything was fine. I was quietly listening, mind wandering in a haze, when I heard it. A voice from behind, speaking in a tone that wasn't meant for me to overhear, but I did.

"Why does she come with her hair open every day?"

And in that instant, the ground beneath me seemed to split wide open. The words didn't just land on my ears, they *pierced* right through me, like a dagger lodged deep in my chest. It wasn't just a comment. It wasn't even just a question. It was an attack. A silent judgment wrapped in casual words, but dripping with venom.

"Why does she…", *as* if my every choice was suddenly on trial. As if something as simple as how I wore my hair was an invitation for criticism.

What they didn't understand and what no one could understand, is that I was already breaking. I was already so fragile, so deeply insecure in my own skin, that every little punch line, every whisper, hit me harder than they could imagine. They couldn't see the cracks in me, couldn't feel how every word, every glance, threatened to make me crumble. I wasn't strong enough to shrug it off.

I wasn't *over* it. I was just running. Running from the past, running from the broken version of myself I couldn't bear to face. I thought I could outrun it. I thought I could silence the self-doubt. But all it took was one careless reminder, one small comment, and suddenly I was back at the starting point. Right back where it all began, drowning in my own insecurities, trapped by the very things I had been trying to escape.

I went home that evening, feeling like a shell of myself. I didn't speak much. I barely looked anyone in the eye. My dad noticed it first. He watched me as I sat silently at the table, not myself. I couldn't hide it from him.

He gently called me over to him, his voice quiet but steady.

"What happened, dear?"

And that was it. That one question was all it took. The floodgates opened, and I broke down. Tears fell uncontrollably as I poured out everything I had kept inside.

"I don't want to go back," I cried.

"They're always talking about me. My looks, my hair… it feels like they're always judging me."

My dad, confused at first, didn't understand why such small things had such a big effect on me. But it wasn't the comments themselves, it was the reflection of my own insecurities, my inability to see myself as anything more than someone who wasn't good enough. I was embarrassed by how vulnerable I have become.

But my dad didn't criticize me for it. He didn't judge me for my tears. He simply held me, reassuring me that this phase would pass, that people would come around.

"It's okay," he said softly.

"They'll understand you, with time. This will be alright."

His words felt like a balm to my wounded heart, and for the first time that day, I felt a little lighter. I decided to give myself time.

Two months. Two months to let things settle, to let me adjust. I kept pushing forward, even when it felt impossible.

I attended events, made a few friends, even started hanging out with a group of people who slowly began to boost my confidence.

But it wasn't an overnight transformation. Even outside of college hours, I found myself sitting alone inside the bus while everyone else chatted away, afraid to meet new people. Not because I was shy, but because I feared the judgment that might follow. The thought that someone, somewhere, would say something about my hair, my face, the way I walked.

And then one day, after weeks of hesitation, I whispered to myself,

"Tanya, it's one day at a time. Just one day."

Slowly, I started working on myself. Every day, bit by bit. It wasn't fast, but it was steady. I told myself I would get better with each passing day.

And just like that, a year passed. One year of small, consistent changes. And in those moments, I began to realize something.

The hardest part wasn't changing my outward appearance, it was finding the strength to believe in myself, to push through the self-doubt, and to realize that I was more than the whispers and comments I had feared for so long.

Chapter 3

Finding My Voice

———— ❖❖ ————

A year had passed, and with it, the ticking of time had somehow intensified. My heart raced in anticipation as my 19th birthday approached. Nineteen. The end of teen and the beginning of adulthood, the gateway to freedom, to *change*. And I was ready for it. I was ready to leave the broken version of 'me' behind, to bury that insecure, frightened girl, and to embrace a new *me*. I thought that with this birthday, the world would open up, and things would finally get better.

But life, it seems, has a way of surprising you.

13th July 2016

Everything felt different. The air was thick with anticipation, but this time, it wasn't just excitement, it was something deeper. It was a sense of *rebirth*. I could feel it in my bones as I entered the house that morning. My family had pulled off a surprise. The living room was alive with color and warmth. Bright pink and purple streamers hung from the ceiling like vines of joy, glimmering in the soft light. The walls danced with golden balloons that floated lazily in every corner, their presence both calming and jubilant.

And the smell... that sweet, intoxicating aroma of cake fresh from the oven filled the room. I could already taste it, rich and comforting. I could see the love in every detail, the hand-made decorations, the tiny sparkling candles flickering on the table, the laughter ringing through the air. My heart swelled with gratitude.

It was perfect. But for once, it wasn't about the cake, the gifts, or the decorations. It was about me. It was about what I had *become*. The world around me was celebrating, but inside, I was reflecting on my own transformation.

Later, after the party had ended and the house had fallen silent, I found myself sitting alone in the living room. The leftover cake sat in front of me - a small piece of sweet comfort. But my thoughts? Well...

What had changed in me?

I stood up from the sofa, holding my slice of cake like a lifeline. I walked slowly to my bedroom and stood in front of the mirror.

The reflection staring back at me was NOT the same one I had seen a year ago. This time, I didn't flinch. I didn't look away. I *studied* myself.

There, in the mirror, was something I hadn't seen in ages - *ME*.

The girl I thought I had lost, the one I had buried under layers of doubt and shame. She was there, staring back at me with silent strength. The Tanya I had left behind was still there, quietly fighting to be seen.

I smiled. It was a small smile at first, like I was testing the waters, but it grew. I realized something then that I hadn't understood before. I had been at war with myself for so long, and now, finally, I was beginning to make peace.

No, I wasn't perfect. Not yet. The battle in my body, the one I fought every day, was far from over. But something shifted within me. I could feel it in the quiet of that room, the way my heart beat stronger, the way I stood taller. I was finally beginning to accept myself. Not fully, but enough.

I made a vow to myself that day. My 19th birthday was not just about celebrating another year of life. It was a declaration:

"I was going to stop hiding. I was going to face the world, no matter how terrified I felt. It was time to put

myself out there. No more letting fear decide my fate. No more sitting on the sidelines."

Step 1 was simple:

Start small. Get comfortable around people. Begin with the little interactions, the thing that scares you the most.

The morning after my 19th birthday, I woke up with a quiet sense of clarity. It was as if the world had tilted just a little more in my favor, and suddenly, everything felt different. For the first time in what felt like years, I had a reason to wake up, something to look forward to every morning.

A new purpose had found its way into my heart, and it filled the emptiness I'd been carrying for so long. I felt a renewed sense of direction, as if the fog in my mind had finally lifted. I understood what I needed to do, and what I had to leave behind. College became the fresh canvas I had been waiting for, a blank space where I could rewrite my story. This was my new beginning, my next chapter.

At first, it wasn't about big leaps. It wasn't about making grand statements. It was about the small victories. The small acts that terrified me, but that I knew would eventually lead to something bigger. I needed to build my confidence piece by piece.

So I began with the basics - Smiling. Not just at my reflection in the mirror but at others. At strangers.

At classmates. The simple act of smiling made me feel lighter, like I wasn't carrying the weight of the world on my shoulders.

Next came the small conversations. Before, I had avoided even the briefest exchange, my mind racing with all the things I could say wrong, all the mistakes I could make. But now, I forced myself to take those first steps.

A "hello" here, a casual comment there. The most terrifying part was the unknown. What if I said something awkward? What if they judged me? But what I soon learned was that most people weren't paying as much attention to me as I had thought. They were caught up in their own lives, just like I was in mine.

I started holding eye contact with people, something I had avoided like the plague. Looking someone in the eye felt like standing on the edge of a cliff. But as I practiced, I realized that genuine connection wasn't as hard to find as I'd feared. I didn't have to be perfect. I just had to show up, even if it was messy, and I learned that people respected that.

In class, I could hear my own voice more clearly in group discussions. I could feel the shift within myself. Before my voice had been a whisper, drowned out by others. But now, I wasn't afraid to speak. At first, my words came out shaky, uncertain. But they came out.

And that, in itself, was a victory. I had learned how to step into the light, even if it was just a flicker at first.

Step 1 became a success.

Not in grand gestures but in these small moments. I started to feel seen. I began to feel like I had a place in the world. I noticed it when I laughed without fear of judgment, when I stood up for myself in a conversation, or when I shared my opinion in class without second -guessing.

It wasn't perfect, but it was real. And it felt like me, not the scared, shy girl I used to be, but someone who was finding her way, slowly but surely.

I could look back and see the tangible growth. The person I was becoming didn't hide behind walls anymore. She stepped out. She smiled more. She spoke her mind. She belonged.

But as successful as Step 1 had been, I knew that the real test, the one that would truly challenge me was still ahead.

Step 2 *The bigger stage:*

"Would I be able to stand in front of a crowd?"

"Would I perform? Would I push past my fears and emerge stronger?"

I didn't know, but I was ready to find out. And that feeling was everything.

I'd learned an important lesson in the past year. When a big opportunity comes your way, don't think. Just do. The longer you sit in your head, the more time you waste, and the more opportunities slip away. So, when the next chance arrived, I didn't hesitate. I acted.

It was a Monday, and the air in the classroom buzzed with excitement. We were no longer the new kids on the block, we were the seniors now, and that alone was enough to make the room feel different. There was a palpable energy in the room as we talked about the incoming freshers. The freshmen, those wide-eyed newcomers. We were their guides now, their role models, whether we liked it or not.

That's when she walked in. A senior, with an air of authority. She carried a clipboard, the weight of decisions in her hands.

"Okay," she said, her voice cutting through the buzz of chatter.

"We need volunteers for Freshers' Day activities. Singing, dancing, and…", she paused for dramatic effect, and my heart skipped a beat.

"…hosting," she finished, the word hanging in the air like a challenge.

My stomach twisted. Hosting. Me? I had never imagined myself on a stage, holding a microphone in front of a sea of people. It was the one thing I was sure I couldn't do.

But then…

Without even thinking, my hand shot up. My heart hammered in my chest as I heard the words come out of my mouth,

"Yes, I'll do it."

The room went quiet. All eyes were on me. The blood drained from my face. What had I just done?

I looked around. No one was shocked. No one was laughing. No one was judging me. Instead, there was a silent understanding in their eyes. They weren't surprised. They were expecting me to step up. Probably, they had already seen something in me that I hadn't seen in myself.

And in that moment, I realized… I had been the only one holding myself back.

I swallowed hard, and suddenly, I was drowning in fear. But I couldn't back out now. There was no turning back. I had to go through with it. I had no idea what I was doing, but I promised myself I would figure it out.

The preparation was a whirlwind. I was given the script, and as I read through the lines, panic set in. The words seemed foreign, like they belonged to someone else. I kept reading them, over and over again, trying to commit them to memory, trying to ease the tension consuming me. But every time I thought I had it, doubt crept in.

"What if I forget my lines? What if I mess up?"

The day of the event had arrived. The air was thick with anticipation, and my nerves were fraying at the edges. I stood in front of the mirror, staring at the anarkali suit hanging from the door. It shimmered under the light like it had a secret to tell me. My heart raced. This was it, the moment I had been preparing for, the moment that would define whether I truly had the confidence I had been working so hard to build.

I stepped into the suit, feeling the delicate fabric against my skin. The weight of it was symbolic, a heavy reminder of all the moments that led me here. As I adjusted the pleats, I felt a surge of nerves twist in my stomach. But I pushed them down.

"I had made it this far. I had worked for this."

With trembling hands, I fastened the last hook and stood straight, looking at myself. The reflection staring back at me was unfamiliar, someone stronger, someone braver. My heart pounded, my palms sweaty, and I couldn't help but notice the way my breath hitched in my chest. I wasn't just dressing up for an event. I was dressing up for a transformation. I was dressing up for a chance to prove something to myself.

The fabric flowed around me like a gentle breeze, its golden embroidery catching the light, making me feel like I was stepping into a world I had only dreamed about. My hair was styled in loose waves, falling around my shoulders, the perfect balance of elegance and simplicity. But as I turned to face the mirror again, a cold rush of fear washed over me.

"What if I stumbled?"

"What if I forgot my words? What if I failed?"

I shook my head, refusing to entertain those thoughts.

"I've endured for this long. I can't back down now."

With one last deep breath, I stepped away from the mirror and walked out. The moment had come. I wasn't just going to stand on stage and speak, I was going to own it. Every step I took toward that stage was a step toward claiming my confidence, toward proving to myself that I could be more than the girl who once hid away in the shadows.

I reached college, stepping out of the college bus, the excitement in the air was overwhelming. Everywhere I looked, I saw people dressed to impress - colors, sequins, and sparkles. The whole campus was buzzing with energy. Friends were greeting each other, laughing, chatting, unaware that in just a few moments, I'd be standing in front of them on that very stage. It felt surreal.

The moment I walked into the auditorium; my stomach dropped. The venue was massive. Rows and rows of chairs stretched out before me, the stage looming high and mighty in the distance. The lights were already bright, the sound system was set up perfectly, and the excitement in the air was thick. I looked around, trying to calm my nerves, but it didn't work.

'I should not have seen this', I thought to myself.

The sheer scale of the setup was overwhelming. So many chairs, so many eyes waiting for me. The massive stage felt like a mountain, and I was a tiny speck standing at the bottom. The butterflies in my stomach suddenly felt like a stampede.

An hour left before the event started. I sat with my friends, trying to force myself to practice my lines. But the anxiety consumed me. I couldn't focus.

My hands were shaking. I looked at the piece of paper in my hand. It seemed like my only lifeline.

I decided I would just read from it, not even try to look at the audience.

I couldn't. *I wouldn't.*

The time was fast approaching. The event was about to begin. My legs felt like they were made of lead. Every step I took towards the auditorium seemed heavier than the last. As we walked in, the noise from the crowd grew louder. I could hear my heart pounding in my ears, louder than anything around me. I tried to steady my breath, but nothing seemed to calm me.

Then came the moment.

The show began, the lights dimmed, and the crowd's energy surged. It was my turn. *My turn.*

My legs felt like they were moving through quicksand. I could feel all the eyes in the room on me. My palms were sweating. I had to step onto that stage. The stage… all eyes on me.

"I can't do this. I can't."

But there I was, at the edge of the stage, the spotlight blinding me. I took my first step, and everything inside me screamed to run. My hands were trembling so badly that I could barely hold the paper. I managed a tight, awkward smile that didn't reach my eyes, and I knew, deep down, it wasn't enough to hide my panic. Each step felt like a hundred kilos, dragging me further into the spotlight, further into the fear I had spent years avoiding.

Then, I did it. I stepped onto the stage, but my gaze never made it to the audience.

"Just don't look at them, Tanya. Don't look at them".

I cleared my throat and spoke into the mic, my voice trembling:

"Hello everyone, welcome to the Fresher's Party 2016. Are you excited?"

The crowd shouted in unison, *"YES, we are!"*

And then, it happened. That was the moment.

That was the instant where something inside me clicked. My gaze slowly lifted from the paper and met the eyes of the crowd. I saw their faces. I saw the smiles, the excitement. They weren't laughing at me, they weren't judging me. They were... with me.

And in that moment, the anxiety began to melt away. It felt like the weight I had been carrying for so long was finally lifting off my shoulders.

I closed the paper in my hand and took a deep breath. And then, I spoke from the heart. No script, no lines, just me. Tanya.

The crowd responded, not with silence or judgment, but with cheers, claps, and loud encouragement. I was doing it. The girl who had feared the stage, who had spent years running from herself, was now standing tall.

The stage - this gigantic, terrifying stage suddenly felt like home. I found myself, and I found my voice. The girl who had been invisible in her own life was now front and center, commanding the energy of the room. I matched the crowd's excitement, building it, amplifying it.

The fear? Gone. Completely gone. I was no longer afraid of the eyes watching me.

The applause still rang in my ears as I walked off the stage, my heart racing in a way that felt electric, like the entire room had shifted around me. I was riding on a high, I hadn't expected a sense of accomplishment, of power, of self. The compliments poured in, each one a wave that lifted me higher.

"You were amazing!"

"You owned that stage!"

Each word felt like a piece of the puzzle clicking into place, and with every compliment, I realized this was the change I had been fighting for. This was the transformation that had always been just out of reach, and now, it was mine.

I wasn't the girl who doubted herself anymore. I wasn't the girl who stayed in the background, shrinking from the spotlight. No, I was the one who had stepped up, who had stood in front of the crowd and owned it. The fear that once paralyzed me had dissipated, replaced by something infinitely more powerful: Belief. The belief that I could do this. That I could show up, unapologetically, and take up space.

From that moment on, I knew things were different. I had taken that first step, and with every step that followed, I knew I would only grow stronger.

I wasn't waiting for permission anymore. I wasn't waiting for the right moment. I had found my voice, and it was loud and proud.

The journey ahead would still have its struggles, its doubts, its setbacks but I was no longer the person who would hide from them. I was ready. Ready for whatever came next, because now, I knew something important:

I could face it.

And that made all the difference.

The hardest part isn't the leap, it's believing you're ready. But once you believe, you realize you always were. And in that moment, you're no longer waiting for your moment -

YOU ARE THE MOMENT.

Interlude

A Quiet Pause

That night, as I lay in bed, the rush of everything still swirling in my mind, I couldn't help but reflect. The moment on stage felt like the beginning of something, something bigger than I could grasp right now. But there was a question lingering in the background, one I couldn't ignore any longer:

Who am I really?

Was this newfound confidence the real me? Was it just a version of myself I'd been hiding for so long? Was I finally stepping into my truth, or was I just trying to convince myself that I had?

It wasn't the first time I'd asked these questions. But tonight, they felt heavier. The world talks a lot about finding yourself, but what happens when you're not sure who you are to begin with? Or when the person you've been trying to be doesn't quite match the person you've become?

The truth is, identity is complicated. It's not a single moment of self-discovery. It's a process. And maybe, in some strange way, the moment I had just lived through was part of my search. But I knew one thing for sure: I wasn't done yet.

And so, the search began.

The truth is, everything I thought I knew about myself was still unfolding. As much as I had stepped onto that stage and made a new promise to myself, there were still pieces of me that I hadn't fully discovered. I was no longer hiding from the world, but that didn't mean I had figured it all out. No, the real journey, the real self-discovery was just beginning.

In the chapters that follow, I'll take you through what I found when I started digging deeper into who I truly was, beyond the surface-level victories. There were moments when I had no answers, and other times when I had to be my own guide, finding my way through the wilderness of self-doubt, fear, and confusion. It wasn't always easy, but each step, each lesson I learned about myself was a piece of the puzzle.

This part of the story, the part you're reading now, is about how I went from a place of uncertainty and fear to a place of gradual strength and clarity. But the story doesn't end here. There's more ahead. Post this discovery, something changed. I started embracing new challenges, stepping into roles I never thought I could.

There were big moments, moments I would have never expected, moments that I would like to share with you from Chapter 12 onward.

So, as you continue reading, you'll witness how this newfound understanding of myself shaped everything that came after. The changes weren't always comfortable, and sometimes, the process felt like I was walking through fire. But as you'll soon see, this journey of transformation led me to places I couldn't have imagined when I first started.

The story doesn't just stop with understanding who I am. What happens after that discovery is what truly redefined my life. Let's continue this journey, and together, let's see what unfolded after I began to truly discover my own worth, my purpose, and my strength.

"This is where the real story begins. What's coming next is not the conclusion of my journey, but the next chapter of transformation."

Chapter 4

Who Am I?

------ ✤✤ ------

The Truth

I didn't have all the answers that night, and maybe I still don't. But as I sat alone in my room, bathed in the soft glow of my desk lamp, a feeling washed over me that I couldn't ignore any longer. The uncertainty, the tightness in my chest, wasn't just a phase, it wasn't a passing mood or the product of sleepless nights. It was something deeper. Something that had a name. **Identity Crisis.**

I had heard the term before, of course. In movies, books, even casual conversations. But I had never truly understood it until now. The word sounded dramatic, almost too big for what I was experiencing. I always thought an identity crisis was a big, earth-shattering event, something that involved wild transformations or radical decisions. But this... this was different. It wasn't a sudden awakening; it wasn't a crisis in the way I expected. It was more of a slow unraveling. A steady erosion of the self.

The person I thought I had become; the confident, unshakable version of myself was beginning to crack. Pieces of it were slowly falling away, and something unfamiliar was taking shape in its place. I couldn't quite put my finger on it. It wasn't better or worse, it was just... different. I felt like I was watching myself change from the outside, unable to stop the process, but unsure whether I should.

This feeling, this creeping sense of something shifting, wasn't just about figuring out who I wanted to be in the future. It was deeper than that. It was a realization that the person I thought I was, the version of myself I had grown so comfortable with, wasn't actually me. It was like standing in front of a mirror and seeing a reflection that didn't quite match the image I had carried for years.

I kept asking myself, *"Is this normal?"*

I had heard that many people experience this sort of confusion, especially in their late teens or early twenties.

A 'phase of transition' that everyone goes through at some point, right? But if it was so normal, why did it feel so difficult? Why did it feel like I was coming apart at the seams?

In my mind, I had always imagined an identity crisis as something more dramatic, something clear-cut. I pictured it as a single defining moment; a sudden revelation. But now I saw that an identity crisis isn't a singular event; it's a process. It's a quiet, almost imperceptible breakdown of everything you once believed about yourself. It's not a loud bang, it's a slow, persistent unraveling, like an old sweater that slowly comes apart at the seams.

And that realization was terrifying.

I began to question everything.

"Who am I really? What do I stand for?"

The life I had carefully built - the relationships, the career path, the goals I had worked towards, suddenly felt hollow. All the things that once defined me now seemed irrelevant. I didn't recognize the person I had become, and the worst part was that I couldn't even pinpoint when it had all started to change.

An identity Crisis happens when the person you've constructed, the version of yourself that you present to the world, no longer fits with the reality of who you are or who you're becoming.

It's the inevitable result of trying to fit into a world that often demands you to be someone you're not. We spend so much of our lives trying to meet the expectations of others; our families, our friends, society that we forget to ask ourselves who we really are when all of that is stripped away.

I wasn't alone in this. I had read about identity crises, heard friends talk about the uncertainty they faced in their own lives, especially during times of transition - graduating, changing jobs, starting new relationships. But in that moment, when everything felt like it was breaking apart, I didn't feel like it was just a "phase." It felt like a crisis. A profound shift that was turning everything I knew about myself upside down. I wasn't sure if I was ready for this, or if anyone ever really is.

But the more I sat with it, the more I understood: it wasn't about fighting the process, it was about accepting that it was happening. An identity crisis wasn't something to fear; it was something I had to embrace, even if I didn't fully understand it yet. It was the only way I would ever uncover the truth about who I truly was.

What caused it? I kept asking myself. What was the root of this crisis, this sudden unraveling?

I thought about the changes that had recently taken place in my life. There had been shifts in my relationships, in how I saw myself, in the way the world saw me. My goals had changed, and so had my values. I wasn't the same person I had been a year ago, or even six months ago. My entire worldview was changing, but I wasn't sure if I was evolving with it.

And then, it hit me:

Change

Change was the catalyst. It wasn't the kind of change that happened overnight, like a new job or a dramatic move across the country. It was more like the gradual erosion of certainty over time. Every small shift, every new challenge, every unexpected experience, it all added up, creating a new version of myself that I wasn't sure I recognized. This process wasn't linear. It wasn't clean. And that's what made it so hard to navigate. I had no clear sense of where I was going or who I would become.

But somewhere deep down, I knew this: the truth I was searching for wouldn't be found in the past. It wouldn't be found in the version of myself I thought I had already figured out. It could only be found in the messy, imperfect process of becoming.

And so, with all the uncertainty swirling around me, I took the first step towards confronting the truth: the truth of who I had been, who I was, and who I might become.

Now that you understand the crisis, ask yourself:

"Is identity something we create, or is it something that's always been within us, waiting to be discovered?

Maybe the real crisis is not the loss of self, but the journey of truly finding it.

Maybe it's time to embark on your own journey of self-discovery ..."

Chapter 5

The Fallout

Effects of Identity Crisis

There wasn't one big moment that changed everything. It wasn't like a sudden revelation or a single event that caused the shift. Instead, it was like the slow fading of light at dusk. The sense of who I was, the person I thought I was, began to fade away bit by bit. With each change, I started feeling like I wasn't fully in control anymore. I felt like I was going through life, but something was off. The ground beneath me had shifted, and every step I took felt uncertain, like I was losing my balance.

At first, I didn't notice much. I went through my usual routine - work, conversations, decisions but there was something nagging at the back of my mind.

Something felt different, like I wasn't the same person anymore. The person I thought I was, confident and sure of herself was slipping away. It wasn't a big crash or dramatic moment. It was just a quiet, slow unraveling.

A Sense of Dissociation: Living in a Parallel World

There were days when I felt as if I was living in two worlds at once. In one, I was physically present, engaging in conversations, attending meetings, going through the motions of daily life. In the other, emotionally, I was detached. It wasn't as if I was consciously pulling away; rather, it was as though I were watching myself from a distance, hearing my own voice and seeing my own actions, but feeling like someone else was controlling them.

I spoke and smiled, but it was mechanical, like I was playing a role in a script I didn't quite understand. I wasn't pretending to be someone else, yet I couldn't shake the feeling that I was wearing shoes that didn't fit, and no one noticed the discomfort.

To the outside world, I was still me. But inside, I was adrift, unable to connect with who I was becoming— or who I had been.

The Silent Anxiety of Uncertainty

Every morning, I woke up to a world that felt both familiar and strange at the same time. The days felt longer, harder to get through. It wasn't just that I didn't know what I was supposed to do with my day, it was deeper than that. I felt a constant, quiet anxiety. I would sink into my thoughts, replaying:

"Who am I? What am I supposed to be doing with my life?"

It wasn't the usual feeling of not having a clear direction, it was a deeper uncertainty about my very identity. It felt like I was waking up from a dream, into a reality I couldn't quite understand.

Every small decision felt huge. Choosing what to eat, where to go, what to wear - they all felt important, like each choice said something deep about who I was. But the harder I searched for answers, the more distant they seemed.

"What did I care about? What did I want? Who was I, really?"

It felt like chasing something that kept slipping away, and the more I tried to find it, the more uncertain everything became.

Emotional Whiplash: The Highs and Lows

Some days, it felt like everything might finally make sense. I would feel a small spark of hope, thinking that maybe I was shedding old layers of myself that weren't truly me, and that I might emerge stronger, more real, more authentic.

But those good days were short-lived. For every high, there was a low. The contrast between the two was sharp, like emotional whiplash. Some days, I felt like nothing mattered. The things I once cared about, felt empty.

I would lie in bed, staring at the ceiling, wondering:

"What's the point of it all?"

My friends seemed to have their lives together, while I felt stuck in my own confusion.

The lows were the hardest. It wasn't just sadness, it was a deep feeling of disconnection. I couldn't connect with myself, so it felt impossible to connect with anyone else. The world seemed to be moving forward, but I was standing still, unsure of where I was headed or what I was doing. It was a constant back-and-forth, and it left me wondering if I would ever feel settled again.

The Disconnection from the Future

There was a time when I looked forward to the future. I had dreams and plans, and I could see my life unfolding in front of me, each step leading to something better. The future was a place of endless possibilities.

But now, it felt distant. The future wasn't the bright, hopeful place it once was. It felt like a big, hollow space, and I wasn't sure if I even wanted to embrace that journey anymore. It wasn't that I didn't have goals anymore, it was more like I couldn't connect with them. Dreams no longer felt exciting or important.

The future, which once felt full of potential, now felt like a void. I didn't know what to fill it with. It felt like I was drifting, unsure of where I was going or why.

Disconnecting from Who I Thought I Was

The hardest part of all this was realizing how much I had changed. The confident, driven person I once was, seemed so far away. I began questioning if the things I used to love, the goals I had worked towards were really important or if I had just been following someone else's idea of who I should be.

It was like I was living someone else's life, and now, with everything unfolding, I was finally seeing the truth: none of it had ever truly felt like me.

I started to feel like a stranger to myself, standing in a room full of mirrors, each one reflecting a different version of me, but none of them felt real. I didn't know who I was anymore without all the labels and roles I had been playing for so long.

A Silent Kind of Grief

Through all of this, there was a quiet grief. It wasn't loud or dramatic, but it was there. I missed the person I had once been - the self-assured, certain version of me. That version of myself now felt fragile.

But I realized something important: this grief wasn't a sign of failure, it was a sign of growth. It wasn't a final goodbye to the person I had been. It was part of the process. It was necessary to let go of who I once was to make room for who I was becoming, even if I didn't know who that was yet. It was a sign that I was changing, and while it was painful, it also brought a sense of freedom.

I had to mourn the past in order to make space for the future. I had to let go of the old version of myself so I could discover who I was truly meant to be. It wasn't easy, and it wasn't clear, but it was the only way forward.

"In the fog, I search for light,
Each step uncertain, yet I fight.
For when the pieces fall apart,
A clearer path begins to start."

A Glimmer of Hope: Embracing the Unknown

As hard as it was to face the uncertainty and grief, I began to realize that this journey wasn't the end. It was just a beginning - a messy, difficult, but necessary step in a bigger journey. I didn't have all the answers, and I didn't know what the future held, but for the first time in a long while, I started to accept the uncertainty. I began to see that maybe I didn't need to have everything figured out.

There was a strange freedom in not knowing. It allowed me to let go of the pressure to be a certain person, to fit into the mold I had created for myself. Slowly, I learned to give myself permission to be unsure, to be in the process of becoming. And in that space, I began to trust that eventually, I would find my way.

It wasn't about finding the "old me," because I was never meant to stay the same. It was about embracing the change, even when it felt uncomfortable. After all, growth doesn't come without discomfort. The person I was becoming wasn't going to be the same as the one I had been, but that was okay. I was learning to welcome the unknown, knowing that it was where true transformation happened.

Chapter 6

The Shifting Landscape

Phases of Identity Crisis

In the midst of all the confusion and pain, there was a quiet sadness. It wasn't loud or dramatic, it didn't come in waves like a storm. Instead, it was subtle, a soft ache that lingered in the background, always there. It wasn't the type of grief you would expect. There were no tears or big emotional outbursts, but it was still grief, just in a quieter form.

I mourned the person I thought I was. The confidence I once had, the feeling that I knew exactly who I was and what I wanted, seemed far away now. It was like that part of me had been slowly taken away, piece by piece, leaving me with only fragments of who I used to be.

The certainty that had once been my foundation now felt fragile. I had built so much of my life on the belief that I knew myself. I thought I understood the world and my place in it. But now, everything I thought I knew was falling apart, and I was left wondering what was real and what was left of me. I stood in the wreckage of my own identity, unsure what to do with the pieces that remained.

Yet, even within the grief, something new started to form. The grief wasn't the end of the story, it was part of the process, a step in the middle of transformation. There was something I needed to let go off, something that no longer fit the person I was becoming. Even though I couldn't see what would fill the empty space, deep inside, I knew it was necessary for growth.

The Loss of a Familiar Identity

The grief felt like losing an old friend, someone I had known for so long, someone who had shaped who I was, even if I hadn't fully realized it. This version of me wasn't perfect, but it was familiar and comfortable. The goals, ambitions, and plans that had once defined me were now starting to feel irrelevant. They were the lens through which I saw myself and the world around me. But as I began to change, I realized those things didn't define me as much as I had believed.

What happens when everything you've built your identity on, begins to fade? What happens when you lose the very foundation that has supported you for years? It's terrifying. It feels like waking up and realizing that everything around you is unstable. The walls you trusted are no longer there to keep you safe, and you don't know what's left.

It wasn't just confusion, it was a quiet mourning. It would hit me unexpectedly, in the middle of my day, when I least expect it.

I would be going about my routine, and suddenly, I'd feel the weight of the loss of something important. Not something I could hold in my hands, but something inside me. A part of my identity had disappeared, and I didn't know how to fill the gap.

The Empty Space Left Behind

As the grief settled in, I started to realize that it wasn't just about the loss of who I was. It was about the empty space left in place of that old identity. I didn't know what to put there. For so long, I had defined myself by external things - my job, my relationships, my goals. But now, all of that seemed irrelevant.

The hardest part was the uncertainty. There wasn't a clear answer for what would fill that empty space. The future, which once felt full of possibilities, now seemed like a blank page with one big question:

"Who do I want to be?"

But in that uncertainty, I began to understand something important. I didn't need to rush to fill the space. The grief had created room for something new. I didn't need to have all the answers immediately. The most important thing was that I was in the process of changing, and that process couldn't be hurried.

The Release: Letting Go of the Old Self

Letting go of the old me was one of the hardest things I had to do. There was a strange resistance within me, as if my old self was holding on tightly, afraid of being left behind. It felt like a tug from the person I used to be, trying to pull me back to what was familiar. But I knew that holding on meant I couldn't move forward.

Letting go wasn't a sudden, dramatic event. It wasn't like a moment of epiphany where everything changed in an instant. It was more of a gradual process, small step by small step. Every time I let go of something I had once believed in, I felt a little lighter, a little freer. It was like peeling away layers of an old identity that had become too tight and uncomfortable.

The more I let go, the more I realized that I wasn't losing myself. I was simply shedding the parts of me that no longer fit, the parts that were based on fear, expectations, and false beliefs. Letting go made space for the person I was truly meant to become. The grief, though hard, was the necessary first step of that transformation. Without it, there could be no rebirth.

The Birth of a New Identity

And then, slowly, things began to shift. At first, it was barely noticeable, but gradually, the empty space that had once seemed overwhelming started to feel less intimidating. The grief didn't disappear, but it became more of a distant memory, reminding me of how far I had come. The weight of the past was still there, but it no longer controlled me.

I began to pay closer attention to myself, listening to what made me feel alive, to what sparked joy and excitement. I started to trust myself again. I made decisions not based on what I thought I should do, but on what felt right in the moment. The future, which had once seemed like a void, started to take shape in a new way. It wasn't the future I had once planned, full of rigid goals. It was a future that felt more open, flexible, and aligned with the person I was becoming.

As I embraced the uncertainty, the grief transformed. It became less about loss and more about growth. The grief was still there, but it didn't scare me anymore. It was a sign that I was evolving, becoming who I was always meant to be.

A New Beginning

In the end, I realized that the quiet grief wasn't something to fear. It was a necessary part of the change. It was the steady rhythm that guided me through the unknown. The grief wasn't the end of the journey, it was the beginning of a new chapter, where I could create a version of myself that was more true, more authentic, and more aligned with who I really was.

Letting go wasn't easy. But in letting go of the old self, I found space for the new. And in that space, I began to rebuild, not a new version of the old me, but something entirely different. Something more real, more free, and more me.

Chapter 7

Breaking Free

A GUIDE TO RECONNECT AND REDEFINE YOURSELF

An identity crisis may shake your world to its core, but it doesn't have to be the defining chapter of your life. While the experience can feel disorienting, it also opens the door for personal growth and transformation. This challenge doesn't have to leave you stuck; it can be the very thing that helps you reconnect with your authentic self.

This chapter will guide you through actionable steps to help you move from uncertainty to clarity. Instead of forcing solutions, you'll focus on creating the space to explore, reflect, and rebuild at your own pace.

It's a journey that requires patience and self-compassion, but with time and dedication, you can emerge more confident, self-aware, and ready to embrace who you truly are.

Embrace the Power of Reflection

The first step towards overcoming an identity crisis is not about immediately changing everything, but about understanding where you are.

Reflection allows you to get in touch with your emotions, thoughts, and the things that have shaped you.

- **Pause and Assess**: Take a moment to stop, breathe, and look inward. Ask yourself,

  "What am I feeling right now? What's been bothering me? What was I like before this all started?"

  These questions help you take stock of your situation and understand where you are in your journey.

- **Journaling**: Writing down your thoughts can be one of the most effective ways to process feelings during a crisis. You don't need to write long, elaborate entries, just a few sentences about your current emotional state can be powerful. Over time, you'll start to notice patterns or recurring themes that will guide you to what's really troubling you.

Reflection is the foundation. You need to understand your starting point before you can make any meaningful changes.

Give Yourself Permission to Evolve

One of the hardest parts of an identity crisis is the fear of letting go of who you were. This fear comes from thinking you're abandoning your past, but in reality, you're allowing room for growth.

- **Release the Old Identity**: Letting go isn't about forgetting who you were, it's about acknowledging that the person you were, doesn't need to define you anymore.

  It's okay to evolve. Who you were yesterday doesn't have to be who you are today, and certainly not who you will be tomorrow.

- **Be Gentle with Yourself**: Transformation takes time. It's crucial to remind yourself that there's no rush. Rebuilding a new identity doesn't require overnight changes.

  Give yourself the space and patience to grow at your own pace, without judgment.

  Letting go doesn't mean losing yourself; it means creating space for who you are meant to become. The person you're evolving into, needs that space to grow.

Reconnect with What Feels Authentic

During an identity crisis, we often disconnect from the things that once brought us joy or made us feel truly alive. This step is about rediscovering those things and reconnecting with what feels authentic.

- **Explore Old Passions**: Think back to activities or hobbies that once made you feel energized or peaceful.

  Whether it's painting, hiking, reading, or writing, reconnecting with your passions will help remind you of the real person within.

- **Try New Things**: This is also a great time to try things you've never done before. New experiences can help you discover parts of yourself that you didn't know existed.

  Whether it's taking up a new sport or volunteering, these activities can spark something new inside you, providing clues about who you're becoming.

  By reconnecting with activities that light you up, you start building a new, authentic version of yourself. The things that excite you can act as a compass in guiding you towards your true identity.

Let Go of External Expectations

A significant reason why identity crises happen is due to the pressure we feel from the outside world - society, family, friends, and even social media. It's time to take a step back and ask:

"What is my *path?"*

- **Question Societal Norms**: We've all been told what success, happiness, and fulfillment should look like. But what if those ideals don't align with who you are?

  Letting go of external definitions of success can help you see your own desires more clearly.

- **Break Free from Other People's Expectations**: You don't have to live up to the expectations of others, your life is yours to create. If certain people or circumstances have shaped your sense of self in a way that doesn't resonate with you anymore, it's time to reframe those influences.

  By letting go of external expectations, you start to reclaim ownership over your identity. You are the only one who knows what's right for you, and it's time to trust yourself.

Be Present and Focus on Small Wins

It's easy to get caught up in the overwhelm of trying to rebuild an entire identity all at once. But you don't need to figure everything out today. Small, manageable steps can bring a sense of control and momentum to the process.

- **Focus on One Thing at a Time**: Instead of trying to solve everything all at once, focus on small, incremental changes.

  It could be something as simple as choosing a new hobby, having a difficult conversation with someone, or setting a goal that excites you.

- **Celebrate Small Wins**: Every time you take a step forward, even if it seems insignificant, take a moment to celebrate. Rebuilding your sense of self is a marathon, not a sprint. These small victories will add up and eventually lead you to the person you are becoming.

  Remember, it's not about how fast you get there, it's about making steady progress and acknowledging the growth along the way.

Surround Yourself with Positive Support

Isolation can make an identity crisis feel even more challenging. Surrounding yourself with people who uplift and support you is crucial in the process of rediscovery.

- **Talk to People Who Understand**: Seek out conversations with friends or family who will listen to you without judgment.

  Sharing your feelings with someone you trust can make a big difference in how you perceive your situation.

- **Join Communities**: Whether online or in person, finding communities that resonate with your journey can be incredibly reassuring. Whether it's groups for personal growth, therapy sessions, or support networks, these spaces can make you feel less alone and more understood.

Having the right people around can provide emotional relief and fresh perspectives. Sometimes, someone else's insight can make all the difference when you're lost in your own head.

Trust the Process

Finally, understand that this journey of rediscovery won't happen overnight. There will be ups and downs, moments of clarity and confusion, but through it all, you must trust the process.

- **Embrace the Uncertainty**: It's okay not to know exactly who you're becoming or what your future holds. The uncertainty you're feeling is part of the process, embrace it rather than fighting it.

You're in the middle of a transformation, and that's something beautiful.

- **Be Patient with Yourself**: Growth takes time. Trust that the person you're becoming is worth the wait. Even when you don't have all the answers, just know that you're heading in the right direction.

Trusting the process is about surrendering to the journey. It's about knowing that even in your darkest moments, something new is taking shape.

This process can feel overwhelming at times, but it's important to stay anchored in positivity. Even when it feels like you're not making progress, remember that change is happening beneath the surface. Each thought, each step forward no matter how small, has the potential to bring you closer to the person you're meant to be.

As you move forward, hold onto the belief that you are becoming exactly who you are meant to be. And to help guide you through moments of uncertainty, remember this mantra:

"I am becoming who I am meant to be, step by step."

Repeat it whenever you feel lost, unsure, or overwhelmed. Let it serve as a reminder that every small step brings you closer to your true self.

Chapter 8

Taking the Leap

Exercises for Personal Growth

Welcome to the Next Phase of Your Journey!

You've been through the hard part: uncovering the truth, understanding the causes, and navigating the challenging phases of your identity crisis. It hasn't been easy, but let's pause and appreciate how far you've come. You've faced the storm, and now, you're standing stronger on the other side.

This chapter marks a new beginning.

Now it's time to take all that introspection, all those realizations, and bring them to life.

This isn't just about theories or abstract ideas anymore. It's about you, in the here and now. This is your moment to step into the future you've been working towards.

It's one thing to understand the process intellectually, but real transformation happens when you take action. You've learned a lot, but now it's time to do something with that knowledge. It's like standing outside after a heavy storm - you've weathered it and now the sky is clearing up, the sun is starting to shine again. And that's where the magic happens.

This chapter is where you reclaim who you are and take ownership of the person you're becoming.

Here's the truth: change doesn't just occur by reading about it. It comes to life when you engage with it, when you dive in and do the work. That's where these exercises come in, they're not just exercises; they're your bridge from understanding to transformation. These activities will speak to your heart and challenge your mind, pushing you to think, reflect, and act in ways that will set you on the path to the future you want.

Are you ready to take that next step?

In the coming pages, you'll find a mix of exercises, prompts, and reflective activities designed to help you not only understand the concepts but to experience the transformation firsthand. Don't rush through them.

These are opportunities for real growth. Take your time, reflect deeply, and most importantly, *do* them. Each exercise is a step towards not just reading about change, but actively creating it in your life. The journey is in the doing and you're already on your way.

Exercise 1

Write Your Story—But With a Twist

We've all got stories we tell ourselves. Some are empowering, some are limiting. What if you could reframe your story from a place of strength?

Take a few minutes and write out the old version of your story, the one you've lived up until now. Include things like:

- What have you believed about yourself?

- How have you defined yourself in the past?

- What old stories have you been holding onto?

Now, here's the twist: Once you've written that, imagine this, what would your story look like if you viewed it from the lens of growth, transformation, and possibility?

Re-write it from that perspective. What would change? How would you describe yourself now, knowing that you have the power to choose a new path?

Tip: Don't overthink it. Just let the words flow. This is about tapping into your new, empowered perspective.

Exercise 2

What's Your New Identity?

In the midst of an identity crisis, it can feel like you're floating in a sea of uncertainty. But remember: you're not lost, you're in the process of becoming.

So, here's a fun and powerful exercise:

- Grab a piece of paper or your phone and write down three words that describe who you used to be. Think about the labels, roles, or identities you've clung to.

- Then, right next to those words, write three new words that describe the person you're becoming. This doesn't have to be perfect, it just has to be real.

Example: Old Identity:

- Stressed

- Overwhelmed

- Stuck

New Identity:

- Resilient

- Free

- Evolving

Don't be afraid to let the words surprise you! And remember, this is 'your' transformation. There's no right or wrong answer. This is a chance for you to redefine yourself in your own terms.

Exercise 3

The Power of "I Am"

Words are powerful. They create our reality. The things we say about ourselves shape how we show up in the world. So, let's work on that.

I want you to spend a few minutes reflecting on the positive qualities you're embracing as you rebuild yourself. Start by writing down 10 positive affirmations or "I Am" statements.

For example:

- I am worthy of love and success.

- I am open to new experiences and learning.

- I am growing stronger every day.

Repeat these affirmations to yourself daily. Stick them somewhere you'll see often: on your mirror, on your desk, or even as your phone wallpaper. Let these statements anchor you as you continue to evolve into your best self.

Exercise 4

Create Your Vision Board (For Real)

Now that you're reflecting on your new identity, let's visualize it. Think about what it looks like to live as the person you're becoming.

A vision board is a powerful tool to manifest your goals and dreams. Here's how you can make one:

1. Gather some old magazines, scissors, and glue or if you prefer digital, use an online platform like Pinterest.

2. Look for images, words, and quotes that resonate with you, things that reflect the version of yourself you're striving towards.

3. Paste or pin them to create a visual representation of your ideal future.

Place your vision board somewhere you can see it every day as a reminder of the life you are creating.

Exercise 5

Challenge Yourself:
30 - Day Transformation Plan

Finally, let's make this personal transformation real. It's time to take action.

Here's a challenge: For the next 30 days, pick one task every day that gets you closer to your true self. It doesn't need to be big, small steps count too.

It could be as simple as:

- Day 1: Practice gratitude by writing down three things you're thankful for.

- Day 2: Do one thing that makes you feel empowered (like saying "no" to something that drains you).

- Day 3: Take five minutes to meditate and clear your mind.

By the end of 30 days, you'll have built new habits and created momentum. You'll be amazed at how these little shifts add up.

Wrapping Up

Congratulations on making it this far. You've already done the hard work, facing your inner challenges, confronting difficult truths, and gaining insights about who you are and where you're going.

The exercises in this chapter weren't just meant to be tasks; they are tools to help you integrate your new understanding into your daily life. This is where the real transformation happens, and it starts with taking action.

Transformation is a process, not an event. It unfolds over time, and sometimes, it will feel slow or uncertain. But that's okay. The key to lasting change lies in the consistency of the small, everyday steps you take.

Each time you show up for yourself, each moment of courage or reflection, brings you closer to the person you are becoming. Trust that the small shifts you make now will eventually lead to big results.

As you move forward, be patient with yourself. Growth isn't linear, and it's easy to become frustrated when things don't happen as quickly as we'd like. But remember, this journey is yours, and it's unfolding at its own pace.

There will be moments of doubt or setbacks along the way, but they don't define your progress. Instead, they are part of the learning process, shaping you into someone who can navigate challenges with resilience and wisdom.

What matters most is your commitment to the path. Every step you take, no matter how small, is a step towards a more empowered, authentic life. So, as you continue forward, embrace the journey with open arms. Stay true to yourself, honor the progress you've made, and allow your vision for the future to guide you.

Remember, the future you're creating is yours to design. It may not look like anyone else's journey, and that's exactly as it should be. The person you're becoming is unique, and that uniqueness is something to celebrate.

As you step into the next phase of your life, know that you have everything within you to create the life you desire.

So take a moment to acknowledge your efforts, breathe deeply, and feel the excitement of what's ahead. The next chapter of your story is ready to unfold, and it's full of endless possibilities. You are ready for this, and the world is waiting for you to step into your power.

Chapter 9

Rollercoaster of Emotions

Riding the Waves of an Identity Crisis

If you've ever felt like your world is turned upside down, like the ground beneath you isn't solid anymore, you're not alone. Going through an identity crisis doesn't just shake your beliefs or thoughts, it shakes you at a deeper, emotional level. You know those days where you wake up feeling completely lost? Where the person you thought you were, no longer feels like you?

That's what happens during this emotional whirlwind, and it's more common than you think.

But here's the truth:

this emotional chaos you're going through isn't something to fight or hide from. It's a signpost on your journey to a new version of yourself. This chapter is all about understanding that emotional rollercoaster, feeling those intense emotions without shame, and knowing that this process will shape you in ways you never expected.

The Emotional Chaos: What You're Really Feeling

When you go through an identity crisis, it's like trying to navigate through a storm. One minute, you feel like you have it all figured out, and the next, you're completely lost. These ups and downs? They're normal. And the sooner you acknowledge them, the easier it will be to move through them. Here's what you might be feeling:

1. Confusion:

The "Who Am I?" Moment

When the foundation of who you thought you were starts to crumble, it's normal to feel lost. You might suddenly question everything: your values, your goals, your relationships. This confusion is the first sign that your old self is making room for something new. It's disorienting, but it's also the beginning of discovery.

2. Existential Dread:

The "What's The Point?" Blues

Ever found yourself staring into the void, wondering what it's all for? That's existential dread, the unsettling feeling that nothing makes sense anymore. It's like everything you've been doing doesn't seem to have a clear purpose. But here's the twist: This is the fertile ground for finding your true purpose. It's messy, but it's real.

3. Sadness and Grief:

Mourning the Old You

When parts of your identity fade away, it can feel like you're mourning a loss. Maybe it's a version of you that's no longer relevant or a dream you've outgrown. Grieving this loss is healthy. It's your heart's way of letting go so you can grow into who you're meant to be next.

4. Frustration and Anger:

The "Why Can't I Just Figure It Out?" Phase

It's frustrating to feel stuck. The anger that comes with it can feel like a tidal wave, you might be angry at yourself, your circumstances, or the people around you. This anger? It's a sign that you care deeply about who you are and where you're headed. It's part of the process, even if it feels uncomfortable.

5. Isolation:

Feeling Like No One Gets It

You might feel alone in this process, like no one truly understands what you're going through. That loneliness? It's an invitation to connect with yourself. And remember: You are not alone in this journey. Many have walked this path before and come out on the other side stronger.

Emotional Recovery: It's Not a Straight Line

Recovery from an identity crisis isn't a smooth ride. It's a winding road full of twists, turns, and sometimes, backpedaling. You won't go through these emotions in a neat, organized way. Instead, you'll find yourself looping through different stages. It's like grieving, it's not a straight line.

1. Denial:

Pretending Everything's Fine

At first, you might convince yourself that this is just a phase, that things will go back to normal soon. But deep down, you know it's more than that. Denial is a shield, protecting you from the overwhelming reality of change. And that's okay, it's part of the process.

2. Anger:

The Storm Inside

As you begin to face the truth, anger can surge. You may feel upset with the world or, worse, with yourself for not having it all figured out. This anger can be intense, but it's also a powerful force pushing you to confront what you've been avoiding.

3. Bargaining:

Searching for Quick Fixes

You might find yourself trying to bargain your way out of the crisis, doing things you think will solve it (like chasing external validation). But this stage is about learning that no quick fix will resolve your inner turmoil. The real answers come from looking inward.

4. Sadness:

Accepting the Loss

As you process what you've been through, sadness can take over. You might feel like you've been abandoned by the version of yourself you once knew. And yes, that's tough. But this sadness marks a turning point, it opens the door to real growth and transformation.

5. Acceptance and Growth:

The Breakthrough

Over time, you'll begin to accept the process. The chaos won't seem so chaotic anymore. You'll find peace in the unknown. Acceptance doesn't mean you have it all figured out, it just means you've learned to be okay with not knowing. And that's when the transformation happens.

Why You Shouldn't Avoid Your Emotions

It's tempting to stuff down all those uncomfortable feelings and "move on" quickly. But here's the catch: Suppressing your emotions won't help you heal. In fact, it'll only delay the process.

Think of emotions like messengers. They're there to tell you something important about yourself. Instead of pushing them aside, welcome them in.

When you allow yourself to feel, really feel, you unlock something powerful. Each emotion whether anger, confusion, or sadness carries valuable lessons that can help you evolve.

And here's the kicker:

The more you face your emotions head-on, the more resilient you become. You learn how to handle tough feelings without letting them control you.

Exercises to Ride the Waves

Here are some ways you can start embracing your emotions, rather than running from them:

1. Journal Prompt:

"What Am I Really Feeling?"

Each day, check in with yourself. Write down whatever comes up - no judgment. Whether it's confusion, sadness, or anger, try to put a name to the emotion. Ask yourself where it's coming from and what it needs.

2. The Body Scan:

Listen to What Your Body's Saying

Sit quietly, close your eyes, and scan your body from head to toe. Pay attention to where you feel tension or tightness. These physical sensations often tie to emotions. Try to connect the physical feeling with the emotion, anxiety might show up in your chest, while stress could sit in your shoulders.

3. Affirmation Exercise:

"I Give Myself Permission to Feel"

Stand in front of a mirror and repeat these affirmations:

"I am allowed to feel all my emotions without judgment."

"My feelings are valid and important."

"I am growing through this process."

Repeat this daily to remind yourself that it's okay to feel, and that those feelings are part of your transformation.

4. Find Your Go-To Coping Mechanisms:

When things get too overwhelming, think about what helps you calm down. Is it a walk in nature? Meditation? Talking to a friend? Get in the habit of using healthy coping strategies, this will help build resilience over time.

The Ups and Downs Are Part of the Process: *Conclusion*

The emotional rollercoaster of an identity crisis is not only natural, it's necessary. The ups and downs you experience? They're part of your growth. And as hard as they are, these emotions will guide you towards a more authentic, powerful version of yourself.

So, instead of fearing them, let them teach you. Lean into the discomfort, ride the waves, and know that this emotional journey is one of the most important steps toward creating the life you truly want.

Chapter 10

Bouncing Back

Build Inner Strength After The Storm

Going through an identity crisis can leave you feeling like you've just been hit by a storm. It's overwhelming, disorienting, and you might feel completely unmoored. You might think,

"Can I ever find my way back to myself?"

It's normal to feel fragile after such a whirlwind. But here's the thing: This isn't the end of your story. It's the beginning of a new chapter, one where you learn to rise stronger, more self-aware, and more resilient than before.

Resilience isn't about pretending everything's fine when it's not. It's not about "toughing up" or avoiding emotions. It's about having the courage to face life's uncertainty head-on and trusting that you have the inner strength to handle whatever comes your way. Think of it as building a muscle, the more you use it, the stronger it gets. You can bounce back from this, and with each challenge, you'll find new layers of strength within yourself.

What is really Resilience?

(And Why It's Your Secret Weapon)

Let's take a step back and define resilience in a way that makes sense for you.

Simply put, resilience is your ability to bend without breaking. It's the emotional muscle that helps you adapt and recover when life throws curveballs, like an identity crisis. It's about finding your footing even when the ground feels like it's shifting beneath you.

Resilience doesn't mean you'll never face struggles again. It doesn't mean everything will magically be easier. It means you'll be better equipped to handle life's ups and downs with more clarity, flexibility, and confidence. Picture it like this: when you strengthen your resilience, you start to flow with life's unpredictability, instead of being swept away by it.

Example:

Think of someone like **Nelson Mandela.**

He spent 27 years in prison, faced unspeakable hardship, and lived through systemic oppression, but his resilience allowed him to emerge not just as a survivor, but as a global symbol of peace and equality.

He didn't just endure, he used adversity as a stepping stone to reshape not only his own life but an entire nation. If he can do it, you can, too.

Tools to Build Your Resilience — RIGHT NOW

Okay, so how do you actually build resilience? It's not something you're born with, and it's not an overnight fix. But with the right tools, you can get stronger over time. Here are some practical strategies you can start using today to help you navigate your IC and come out even more empowered:

1. Mindfulness:

Your Superpower in the Chaos

Mindfulness is the practice of being fully present in the moment - no judgment, no rushing. It's about noticing what's happening right now without getting caught up in the past or future. This simple habit can be a game-changer when everything feels out of control.

Try this:

When things feel overwhelming, take a moment to breathe. Close your eyes, take a deep breath, and focus on the sensation of the air entering and leaving your body. This simple practice can immediately ground you and reduce anxiety.

2. Cognitive Reframing:

Turning Setbacks into Comebacks

Life is full of obstacles. But how you perceive them shapes your experience. **Cognitive reframing** is the art of changing how you look at challenges, it's not about ignoring the struggle, but about finding growth in it.

Try this:

Next time you're feeling stuck or overwhelmed, ask yourself:

"What can I learn from this?" or *"How is this challenge making me stronger?"*

Changing your mindset can be the difference between feeling defeated and feeling empowered.

3. Positive Self-Talk:

Rewriting Your Inner Script

The way you speak to yourself matters. If you're constantly telling yourself that you're not good enough or that you'll never get through this, those negative thoughts can become a self-fulfilling prophecy. But by practicing **positive self-talk**, you can rewire your brain to think more kindly and constructively.

Try this:

Every morning, stand in front of the mirror and say things like,

"I'm strong", "I'm learning every day," or "I can handle whatever comes my way."

The more you affirm these truths, the more you'll believe them.

How to Build Resilience Every Day – LITTLE BY LITTLE

The thing about resilience is that it's not a one-time fix. It's a daily practice, just like brushing your teeth. If you make these habits a part of your routine, you'll build mental and emotional muscle that will help you face even bigger challenges in the future.

1. Start a Gratitude Journal:

When life feels heavy, it's easy to focus on everything that's wrong. But focusing on what's going right, even the small stuff can make a big difference. Gratitude shifts your focus from scarcity to abundance, and over time, it rewires your brain to notice the positive.

Try this:

At the end of each day, write down three things you're grateful for. It can be as simple as a good cup of coffee or a kind word from a friend. This small habit can change your perspective on life.

2. Push Yourself Outside Your Comfort Zone:

Growth doesn't happen in your comfort zone. Every time you challenge yourself to try something new, you stretch your emotional limits and build resilience.

Try this:

Pick something that scares you a little. It doesn't have to be huge, maybe you sign up for a class you've been avoiding, or initiate a conversation you've been putting off. Every time you step into discomfort, you're building your inner strength.

3. Self-Compassion:

Be Your Own Best Friend

Resilience doesn't mean being hard on yourself. In fact, the opposite is true. Being kind to yourself when things don't go as planned can help you bounce back faster. Think of how you'd comfort a friend in the same situation.

Now, do that for yourself.

Try this:

The next time you make a mistake, say to yourself,

"I'm doing the best I can. I'll learn from this, and I'll do better next time."

Self-compassion will speed up your recovery and make you more resilient in the long run.

Reflection Exercise: Recognize Your Strengths

Sometimes, you need to take a moment to look back at how far you've come. By reflecting on the challenges you've already faced, you can remind yourself of just how strong you truly are.

Here's an exercise to help you do that:

1. List Past Challenges:

Think back to a time in your life when you faced something difficult. Maybe it was a breakup, a job loss, or a personal struggle.

Write down at least three challenges you've overcome.

2. Identify How You Managed:

For each challenge, ask yourself how you got through it. Did you rely on your emotional strength? Did you seek support? Did you change how you thought about the situation? Write it down.

3. Strengths Assessment:

Look at your list of challenges and strengths. Reflect on what those experiences taught you.

What coping strategies did you use that you can apply now? Recognizing your resilience will help you face your Identity Crisis with more confidence.

Wrapping It Up

Resilience Isn't About Avoiding the Storm, It's About Dancing in the Rain

Life doesn't stop throwing challenges your way, but resilience is about learning how to weather the storm. It's not about avoiding pain, but about learning how to face it, grow through it, and ultimately become stronger for it.

So, take a deep breath, know that you have everything inside you to overcome this, and start building your resilience today. Every little step counts, and the more you practice, the stronger you'll become. The storm may be wild now, but in time, you'll find the strength to dance through it.

Interlude

Gentle Reminder

If you're reading this and feeling like you're standing in the middle of your own transformation, know that you're not alone. Change is hard, and letting go of who we thought we were is never easy. But it's also an opportunity, a chance to rebuild, reimagine, and rediscover who we truly are. So, as you move forward in your own journey, be gentle with yourself. Trust that the space you're in right now, uncertain as it may feel, is exactly where you need to be to grow into the person you are meant to become.

Chapter 11

Reflections of a New ME

The Turning Point

The end of my second year felt like the aftermath of a storm. For months, I had been running after a version of myself that wasn't truly mine. I had been consumed by trying to meet everyone else's expectations, to match the ideal version of success that everyone around me seemed to have.

I spent too much time trapped between who I was and who I thought I should be, constantly comparing myself to others, and trying to outrun my own insecurities.

But it wasn't until I started diving into sessions focused on self-awareness and identity (I've accumulated the readings from Chapter 7 - 11), that the chaos in my mind finally began to calm. Slowly, everything started to make sense. It felt like pieces of a puzzle, previously scattered and disjointed, had suddenly clicked into place.

For the first time, I could name the confusion I had been living with, for so long. I wasn't lost; I had simply been blinded by fear, by expectations, by the noise of the world around me. The fog began to lift.

I didn't have all the answers, but I felt like I was no longer walking blindly through life. I wasn't alone in this struggle, and the realization, that I wasn't the only one grappling with these feelings gave me a sense of peace I had long forgotten.

Looking at myself in the mirror, I felt something I hadn't felt in years: acceptance.

It wasn't perfect; it was raw, unfinished, a work in progress, but it was a start. The weight of years of insecurity began to feel lighter. Slowly, I was starting to build a sense of self, one piece at a time.

The initial excitement of Freshers' Day, the buzz of starting something new had long faded into the background. Now, my life had become quieter, more reflective.

But even in the stillness, the question that had haunted me for so long finally began to make sense:

Who am I really?

I wasn't just a stranger in my own life; I was on a journey of discovery.

I began focusing on myself;

Physically, Mentally, and Emotionally.

Every small step forward felt like a personal victory, like I was rediscovering the parts of me I had forgotten. I had been so out of touch with my own self, so disconnected from my body. I started to gain weight, not in a self-destructive way, but in a way that felt right.

Food, once a source of fear, became a source of nourishment. I ate. And ate. It was like I had been starving for so long, I didn't know when to stop. I joked about being a pig, but the truth was, I didn't care.

The judgments, the stares, the scale, none of it had power over me anymore. I wasn't obsessed with perfection. I was more focused on progress. Sure, I still cared a little, but it no longer consumed me. For the first time in years, I felt free.

But even with all this growth, I knew the journey wasn't over. I wasn't completely confident yet. I was still searching for that part of me that felt whole - complete. I had come so far, but I was far from being done.

Then, the final semester of my second year arrived, carrying with it a strange mixture of hope and uncertainty. The possibilities stretched out before me, but so did the doubts. And just as I thought I had found my rhythm, everything changed.

It was just another ordinary day, or so I thought. The usual hum of chatter, the sound of laughter, the debate over the latest movie no one had actually seen. But today, something was different.

There was an energy in the air, an undercurrent of anticipation that I couldn't quite place.

Then, she entered. A faculty member, but there was something different about her today. She walked into the room with purpose, her presence cutting through the noise.

The room went quiet instantly.

"Students," she said, her voice commanding, *"Please head to the auditorium after lunch. We have something important to discuss."*

Curiosity buzzed in the air. What was going on? Was it a guest lecture? A new announcement? Something big?

After lunch, we made our way to the auditorium, speculation buzzing between friends. As I entered, I noticed a few unfamiliar faces at the front. Professionals, not students.

The room felt different today. This wasn't just another random lecture. This was important.

The screen flickered to life. The first slide appeared. But it wasn't the words that caught my attention, it was the logo.

ISB

Indian School of Business.

My heart skipped a beat.

ISB? *Here?* In our college?

I had always heard about ISB, the prestigious institution that seemed worlds apart, reserved only for the elite, the top-tier students who had the right pedigree, the right connections. And here it was, in front of me.

My pulse quickened. My breath caught in my throat.

Could someone like me really belong in a place like ISB?

I nudged my friends, trying to hush them. They thought I was being dramatic, but they didn't get it. This wasn't just another guest lecture.

This was huge.

The speaker, poised and confident, started explaining the details of the two-year program. She talked about the rigorous selection process, the criteria, the competition.

"Only 18 slots across all branches", she said.

18 students out of 2,000.

My heart plummeted. My doubts flooded in instantly:

"Could someone like me even dream of being selected?"

"Could someone who had always been too afraid to step outside her comfort zone, who had always been labeled as "ordinary," even stand a chance in a place like this?"

"No," I thought.

"This isn't for me."

But then, like a flicker of light in a dark room, a small voice whispered inside me:

"What if?"

The inner battle began. It was like two versions of me were standing face-to-face, arguing fiercely.

One was calm, confident, and fearless. The other was filled with self-doubt, insecurity, and hesitation.

It was a fight between hope and fear.

"Tanya, what do you have to lose? Just try. What's the worst that could happen?" the hopeful voice urged.

"But I don't belong. I'll fail. I'm not one of them. I'm just... ordinary," the voice of doubt retorted, frantic and unsure.

"Why does it matter what they think? Why not you?" Hope countered, soft but unwavering.

And in that moment, the tide shifted. My doubt began to fade, and a quiet confidence settled within me. I didn't know if I would succeed, but I knew I had to try. So, despite the fear, despite the voice of doubt screaming in my head, I applied.

What followed was unexpected. My friends, the ones I thought would mock me for even dreaming of such a thing, followed suit. They applied too.

Together, we took a leap into the unknown, daring to defy the odds, to dream bigger than we ever had. And for the first time, I felt a sense of freedom I hadn't felt before.

Days turned into weeks, and the wait became agonizing. Every day that passed, I grew more certain that I wouldn't make the cut. The excitement that had surrounded the program started to fizzle out. Everyone moved on. But then, a month later, in the middle of an ordinary afternoon, a call came.

The Placement Head.

My heart skipped a beat.

"Why is she calling me? I'm just a second-year student."

I walked into the placement office, a space that felt foreign and tense. Students sat there, calm and collected, the ones everyone expected to make it.

Confident. Well-known.

The ones who seemed destined for success. I couldn't help but wonder what I was doing there.

Then, we were called into the conference room. As I stepped in, the room went still. And then, she walked in.

The Placement Head.

She had a way of commanding attention, of making the entire room fall silent with just her presence.

She didn't need to raise her voice to be heard.

"Congratulations," she said, her voice calm, but full of authority.

"You have all been selected for the ISB program. You are the 18 students chosen from this college."

'Time stopped.

"Me?"

The weight of the moment hit me like a wave. In that instant, I felt a surge of something powerful, something I had never felt before.

Confidence.

It wasn't just about getting into a prestigious program, it was about something deeper. It was about realizing that I wasn't ordinary. I was worthy.

Looking around the room, I realized I was the only one from my department.

I was the one.

In that moment, things took a turn. I had made it.

But I didn't stop there. The fire inside me grew brighter. I started pushing myself even harder, taking on new projects, participating in massive events, leading teams, presenting papers.

The ISB program exposed me to a whole new world - entrepreneurship, pitching ideas, collaborating with students from other top colleges. It was transformative.

When I graduated, I was no longer the same person who had walked into college. I was unrecognizable - confident, unstoppable, and proud of the journey I had taken.

Out of the 18 who had been selected, only 8 of us made it to graduation. And I was one of them.

"I made it!" I shouted, my heart swelling with pride.

Not only had I made it, I had *stood out*. People knew my name. They respected me.

For the first time in my life, I felt like I belonged.

And I didn't stop there. I kept pushing. I kept dreaming. I kept striving for more. Because now, I knew:

I belong here.

I am limitless.

And nothing, nothing can stop me.

Chapter 12

Letter to the Girl I left Behind

Hey, you.

Yeah, I'm talking to you, the version of me who's standing in the middle of a storm, drowning in doubt, struggling to stay afloat. I know what it's like to feel lost, to look in the mirror and see a stranger staring back at you.

A stranger who doesn't feel like they belong anywhere.

A stranger who's fighting to be something they're not, thinking that's the only way to survive. I see the exhaustion in your eyes, the endless pressure weighing you down, the fear of falling apart, and the persistent belief that you'll never be enough. I feel that ache, that pain.

But listen to me when I say this:

"You are not broken. You are not lost. You are not invisible."

You're just so caught up in the expectations around you, trying to fit into the mold everyone else has carved, that you can't see the fire inside you.

The strength you've been hiding. The courage you're afraid to unleash. I know you're terrified to step out of the shadows, worried the world will laugh at you, reject you, judge you.

But let me tell you something you don't want to hear right now:

"The world doesn't get to define you. You define yourself."

You're standing in the middle of this mess, convinced you're failing, thinking you're too far gone to fix.

But hear me out:

Every struggle, every tear, every second of doubt is leading you to something bigger. Something more powerful than you can even imagine.

The person you're terrified to become - the messy, raw, imperfect version of you, that's the one who will change everything. You don't have to be perfect. In fact, perfection is a lie.

The world will never let you be who it says you should be. But the moment you stop trying to be everyone else is when the magic happens. That's when you start living.

Right now, you're clinging to fear like it's your lifeline, but it's slowly drowning you.

You're paralyzed by the idea that you'll never be enough, but the truth is:

You are more than enough. You are so much more than the labels they've stuck on you. You are bigger than the tiny box you've been trapped in.

There's an entire world out there waiting for you to stop hiding, to stop holding back, to stop fearing the unknown.

You don't know it yet, but you're about to walk through fire. You'll face things you never thought you could survive.

And every scar, every bruise, every breakdown will build you into someone stronger than you've ever dreamed of becoming. It won't be easy. It will break you. It will shake you.

But that's the point - you can't grow without breaking.

You'll question everything. You'll feel like you're failing with every step. You'll want to give up, crawl into the hole you've dug, and never come out. But the moment you quit is the moment you lose. And you, my friend, are not a quitter. You are a fighter.

Do you even realize how powerful you'll be when you stop listening to that voice telling you, you're not enough? When you stop hiding and start living unapologetically?

When you see that failing isn't the end, but part of the process? That's when you will truly come alive.

You're not stuck. You're not broken. You're in the middle of your transformation.

So, stop letting fear control you. Stop letting the belief that you don't belong, hold you back. You belong.

Not because anyone else says so, but because you say so. The minute you start believing in yourself, the world will start believing in you, too. And I'm not talking about some fairy-tale fantasy.

This is real. This is happening. But it's not going to happen until you stop doubting your worth.

Right now, it feels impossible to see it. The storm seems endless, but trust me, you're the one who created it. And you're the only one who can calm it.

You're going to rise from this. You'll look back one day and laugh at how small those fears once seemed. You're going to walk into rooms you never thought you'd belong in and take up space. You'll be the one everyone notices because you dared to be real. You dared to live your truth.

And guess what? You're going to make it. You'll achieve things you once thought were impossible. You'll conquer dreams that were too big for you to even imagine. But none of that will happen until you start believing in yourself, right now, at this very moment.

So, stop running away from your potential. Stop being afraid of who you're meant to be. And when the world tells you that you don't fit in?

Smile.

Because you were never meant to fit in. You were born to stand out.

You're going to be a force. You just have to believe it.

I believe in you, even if you don't believe in yourself yet. Trust me, you'll get there. And when you do, you'll look back at all the times you thought you were too small, too weak, too invisible, and you'll laugh. Because you'll realize you were never any of those things.

You were always destined to be great.

With all the love,

The Future You

Chapter 13

This is ME, Unapologetically

Today, if there's one thing I know for certain, it's the immense power of authenticity. In a world that demands perfection at every turn, I've chosen to stand tall with my flaws, my quirks, my real self. Whether it's online or face-to-face, I've stopped hiding behind filters, behind façades.

There's something oddly liberating about showing up as the person I truly am; no masks, no pretenses. And you know what? People actually respect it.

Authenticity isn't just accepted - it's magnetic.

When you stop pretending, the world starts to see you for who you really are. And that? That's when the magic happens.

What I've come to realize is this:

It's no longer about chasing the ideal version of myself. It's about embracing who I am right now, flaws and all, and striving to grow with every new day.

Gratitude has anchored my life. I wake up each morning, thankful for the opportunities, the people, and the lessons life throws my way. And at the end of each day, I carve out a moment to reflect, to plan, to meditate, to manifest good things not just for me, but for others, too.

I've become a believer in the law of attraction.

Life isn't always a straight path, but I try my best to stay optimistic, even when the road ahead seems unclear. Sometimes, just holding on to that spark of positivity is the one thing that can keep you moving forward.

I won't lie and say I'm free from anxiety or stress.

Honestly, who is?

But today, I know myself better than ever before. I no longer shy away from challenges.

Instead, I face them head-on.

That's why I've become a Certified Mental Health Mentor. I help those who are weathering their own storms, and I do it because I want to be the person I once needed.

A listener. A friend. A safe space.

It brings me joy beyond measure to know that I can provide that for others.

Confidence, too, has been a muscle I've worked tirelessly to build. Public speaking, hosting - things that once terrified me have now become second nature.

Whether I'm hosting an event or leading a group, I no longer second-guess myself. I'm not the quiet observer I once was. I'm now the one standing in front of the crowd, owning every moment.

I'm evolving from a follower into a leader. And that shift?

It's been nothing short of transformative.

This book?

It's my heart laid bare. My truth, raw and unfiltered. I'm done hiding, done pretending. I'm ready for whatever comes next - the judgment, the praise, the silence, or the applause.

I'm here, giving you all a glimpse of the real me.

And here's the thing:

I don't care if you love me or hate me. This is my journey. My truth.

And I'm no longer afraid to share it.

Empathy has become my compass. Respect is no longer a choice, it's a way of life. The more I give, the more I receive. I've learned to truly understand others, and in turn, they've learned to understand me.

I'm deeply grateful for the support I've received along the way from my family, my friends, my colleagues, even my acquaintances. Their encouragement means more than they'll ever know.

And to those who doubted me? Who didn't believe in me? I thank you too.

Your skepticism became my fuel. Every moment of doubt you cast upon me only strengthened my drive to prove that I'm capable of more than you ever imagined.

The future won't be perfect, and I'm not naive enough to think it will be. But it excites me. I'm eager to keep growing, to keep learning, to keep pushing myself beyond what I thought was possible.

I know there will be more obstacles, but now, instead of running from them, I'm walking towards them, ready for whatever comes next.

If you're reading this and you feel lost, or if you're not yet where you want to be, just know this:

You are not alone.

Your story is still unfolding, and every step forward, irrespective of how small, matters. Keep going. Keep believing.

The best parts of your journey are ahead of you. So, don't stop now.

What if the real magic isn't in the destination, but in the journey itself?

Every misstep. Every heartbreak. Every victory.

These are the moments that carve us into who we're meant to be. And today, I'm not merely surviving, I'm embracing life with everything I have.

I'm not waiting for the world to hand me the perfect moment;

I'm creating it, with every choice, every challenge, every heartbeat.

If, by now, you've created an image of who I am in your mind, I'd love to hear it. This book has been my truth, my vulnerability, my essence on every page.

And now, as you turn to the last page, you'll find me - not just in words, but in the person standing here, unapologetically, fully, and completely... ME.

This is where the story ends, but you can always find me in the real world, with no filters, no masks.

Just... me, as I am.

And so, this chapter closes. And with it, the journey I've shared with you comes to an end.

But the story?

It's only just the beginning.

The End.

Through every storm, I've learned to dance,
In every shadow, found my chance.
I'm no longer who I used to be,
I've become the person I was meant to be.

Chapter 14

Outtakes...

Deleted Scenes from my Journey

Scene 1 - The "I'll Start Tomorrow" Epiphany

It was 3:45 AM, I had just finished a three-hour Netflix binge, and I found myself having the *greatest* realization of my life. I was lying there, thinking, "Tomorrow, I'll be a brand-new version of me. I'll be healthier, more focused, and definitely less obsessed with my couch."

Spoiler: Tomorrow came, and I hit snooze six times instead of hitting my goals.

Scene 2 - The Failed Meditation Session

I decided to try meditation. I sat cross-legged, eyes closed, and took a deep breath and then another and another...

until my mind was suddenly racing with all the things I *wasn't* doing.

"Did I lock the door? Did I text back my friend? What was that weird sound in the kitchen?" Ten minutes later, I opened my eyes, realizing I hadn't meditated at all. I had just performed a mental marathon of "what-ifs."

Spoiler: I didn't find inner peace.

Scene 3 - The Day I Thought I Could Be a Perfect Leader

I walked into a meeting thinking, *"I'm going to own this. I'm a leader now."* And then, halfway through, my voice cracked like I was 13 again, and I accidentally knocked over my water bottle in the most dramatic way possible, spilling it all over my notes. But you know what? I didn't let it stop me. I smiled, said, *"This is fine,"* and continued on. Just a little *perfectly imperfect* moment for the record.

Scene 4 - The "Confidence Boost" That Turned Into a Confidence Crash

So, I decided to take a leap and sign up for public speaking. *"How hard could it be, right?"* Well, let's just say my first attempt involved forgetting every single word I had prepared, awkwardly standing in front of a crowd of people who were *definitely* wondering if I had eaten too many snacks beforehand. There was a moment where I considered just walking off the stage, but I didn't. Instead, I ended up making a joke about it, and guess what? The crowd loved it.

Moral of the story: Sometimes confidence comes after the crash.

Scene 5 - **The Impromptu Dance Party to Break the Tension**

Sometimes, in the middle of a challenging day, the only thing that helps is a little dance party. But when I tried it, I didn't expect the entirely uncoordinated, flailing mess that occurred. I looked like a windmill during an earthquake, flopping around like a fish out of water.

Was it graceful? No. Did it help? Absolutely.

At least I got some good laughs out of it (and maybe a few bruises, but that's another story). So, yeah, dancing for the soul might not look graceful, but it sure as heck feels freeing!

That's a wrap!

But you can always turn back to page one

(or)

Find me right here.

'Hey there,

I'm no longer the person I was when I started this book, and neither are you. Together, we've moved forward- through doubts, struggles and growth. This journey was about embracing change, not perfection. I hope you see that growth in yourself too."